FLAT RACING FOR PROFIT

by Peter May

ISBN: 0 900611 74 X

Raceform Ltd.,
Compton, Newbury, BERKSHIRE RG20 6NL.

Front Cover Picture: Gerry Cranham
Edited: Graham Wheldon

ACKNOWLEDGEMENTS

Many thanks to Sara Howes, Andrew Parsons, Colin Proffitt, David Rossiter and Richard Lowther for their proof-reading skills and suggestions for the content of this book.

Published: Raceform Ltd., Compton, Newbury,
BERKS RG20 6NL.
Printed by: Alden Press, Hawksworth, Southmead Industrial Park, Didcot, OXON OX11 7EN.

CONTENTS

LIST OF TABLES

INTRODUCTION

"It's the most enjoyable way to make a living there is." Little did I know at the time, but these words were to change my life in the most radical fashion. Back then I was working in one of the less glamorous jobs in racing, and was desperate to find a career that offered a greater element of job satisfaction.

By March 1995 I had released myself from the mundane routine of 9 to 5 employment and joined a select group of people who simply bet for a living.

The influence which had such a dramatic effect on my lifestyle was that of a fellow professional gambler whom I shall refer to as John. John is one of the major players; his main problem is finding a bookmaker to bet with, whereas mine is finding a horse to bet on. John is quite simply a master craftsman. He is, in my opinion, the best judge of a horse's potential there is. Simply by watching a horse run he is able to determine its optimum racing conditions, and to pinpoint any potential weaknesses.

As an example, consider the case of Callisoe Bay. In early 1995, Callisoe Bay was considered to be the best 2 mile novice hurdler in training. This was based on two impressive wins at Wetherby and Newbury, by an aggregate of 30 lengths. It was even debated whether he should miss the top novice events at Cheltenham and instead race in the Champion Hurdle, so highly was he considered. Before his third race, at Sandown, I discussed his potential with John, and informed him that I thought the horse was an absolute certainty. The betting supported this view with Callisoe Bay at 1/2 and his nearest rival, Silver Wedge, a good novice trained at the time by David Nicholson, priced at 4/1. "I'm a little worried", John replied, "I can just see him being caught in the last 200 yards." Now, Sandown has a stiff uphill finish, and after leading throughout the race it was whilst climbing this hill that Callisoe Bay was indeed caught by

Silver Wedge, and passed. I stood open-mouthed, how did he know?

This is just a hint of John's ability. However, coupled with this talent for horse-watching, he possesses an extensive knowledge of the form book, a phenomenal memory and, probably most important of all, an acute awareness of value. To John price is everything. This is a concept that punters, myself included, find most difficult to grasp. For John to have a bet the price must be right. I have seen him ignore the horse he thinks is the most likely winner and instead back a different horse in the race simply due to price.

Whilst the main aim of this book is not to dissect the analytical processes of a professional gambler (even if this could be achieved), I will be using a great deal of information gleaned from John and other colleagues to illustrate to the reader the issues which need to be considered when assessing horses for betting purposes. For instance, the concept of value in betting, the importance of previous race times and the effect of the draw.

Many hundreds of books have been written promising the reader that it is possible to make a fortune from betting on racing. The majority adopt a standard form. Detailed explanations are given regarding the configuration of the racecourses, and the importance of making sure your selection is suited by the race distance and going, has good recent form, is trained at a top stable and ridden by a top jockey. Quite honestly, while this is good solid stuff it is rather disappointing to read it again and again in almost every racing book when all the while hoping to find a new, innovative approach to racehorse selection. I will make a guarantee to the reader that he/she will not have to dredge through pages of tenuous, woolly comments of the *make sure the horse is suited by left handed tracks* kind in this book.

At the risk of upsetting the traditionalists, I would go so far as saying that the conventional approach to racehorse selection will only lead to a long term loss. On average the bookmaker bets to an over-round of about 30% (see Part I) and has at his/her disposal all the information available to the general public. So in order for the punter to return a long term profit the bookmaker has either to display appalling judgement, or the punter needs to be so accurate at analysing the race and converting the findings to true probabilities that he/she can turn this huge loss into a positive gain.

Naturally, off-course punters can take early prices (on about 30% of races) or early shows in an attempt to beat the book, but the margin of loss is so great that, in general, it is still unlikely they will make a profit. After all John's profit is only between 10p and 15p per £1 staked, and that is with zero tax since he only bets on-course.

An alternative is to adopt an unconventional approach to racehorse selection. This book is the result of the analysis of tens of thousands of races with the sole aim of identifying profitable betting approaches that differ from the conventional theory.

In Part I some general issues relating to Flat racing in Great Britain are outlined before a detailed investigation into several strategies for highlighting potentially profitable juvenile runners is presented. This is followed by an examination of non-juvenile horse races where special attention is paid to the use of race times, previous race details and the effect of the draw. Part II considers several issues concerning bets and betting. An examination of the concept of value in betting is followed by a comparison between each way and win only betting strategies. Win only Tote betting is then suggested as a value alternative to starting price betting under certain conditions, and the section ends with a look at forecast betting.

Notation

Throughout this text the following notation will be used to illustrate returns from a number of bets: six bets with two winners at 3/1 and 5/1 would be summarised as follows:

Bets	Wins (%)	Return/£
6	2 (33.3)	0.67

In the above example, the six bets produced a return of £4 to a £1 stake (i.e. +3+5-1-1-1-1 = 4), therefore the average return per bet is 4 ÷ 6 (total return divided by the number of bets) = 0.67. It should be noted that a return of 0.09 would simply be sufficient to cover the cost of tax (at 9%), anything less would result in a loss. Finally, all bets referred to throughout this book are win singles unless otherwise stated.

PART I

SELECTION METHODS FOR FLAT RACING

SELECTION METHODS FOR FLAT RACING

Ah, what dusty answer gets the soul
When hot for certainties in this our life.

G Meredith (1909)

The turf Flat racing season in Great Britain starts in late March and ends in early November. Recently it has been supplemented by *all weather* racing and Flat racing now runs through all twelve months of the year. In 1996 the number of racecourses in Great Britain totalled 59, and more than half of these will share about 4500 Flat races scheduled to take place during the year.

These four and a half thousand races can be categorised in several different ways, one of the most convenient of which is age. Two-year-old horses (juveniles) do not start racing until the start of the turf season in late March. Approximately 24% of all races are confined to juvenile horses. Non-juvenile horses, those of three years and upwards, contest the remaining 76% of races. This age distinction is very important in Flat racing. Only a handful of races each year allow juveniles to compete against older horses. Therefore, these two age groups can be analysed entirely independently.

An alternative categorisation can be made by considering the type of race. Roughly 49% of all races are handicaps (known as nurseries if confined to two-year-old horses only). The main difference between handicaps and non-handicaps is that in the case of handicaps each horse is assigned a different weight to carry by a team of

Handicappers employed by the British Horseracing Board (BHB). The aim is to give all horses the same chance of winning by penalising the better animals by giving them more weight to carry. Consequently, these races are usually more competitive than non-handicaps, and thus harder for the punter to assess. However the prices offered by the bookmakers should be higher to compensate for the extra degree of difficulty.

Races may also be broken down by race distance. Races over 5 and 6 furlongs (1 furlong = 1/8 mile) are known as sprints, whilst those of over 14f are referred to as stamina races. The distribution of races by race distance is given below:

Race Distance (f)	**5-6**	**7-9**	**10-13**	**14+**
Percentage of Races	30.9	36.0	25.7	7.4

Due to Britain's unpredictable weather, and the fact that the majority of races are run on turf, the underfoot conditions on which the horses race (*going*) can vary from meeting to meeting. The going is classified into 7 categories: Hard (the driest, firmest ground), Firm, Good to Firm, Good, Good to Soft, Soft and Heavy (the wettest, softest ground). There are a further two classifications for all weather surfaces: Fibresand and Equitrack. The all weather tracks at Southwell and Wolverhampton are constructed from Fibresand, whereas the artificial surface at Lingfield is an Equitrack surface.

Clearly, Flat racing is very varied in this country offering the punter a wide choice of race types over different distances on which to bet. Whilst this variability may offer the punter a certain amount of entertainment value, a more important issue is: how does racing compare to other forms of gambling with respect to return per bet? Backing every horse in every race would, as expected show a loss. In fact, backing every horse in the last 18,000 races would show a loss of 32p per £1 staked, and that's before tax. What about the lucky pin approach? Selecting a horse at random in the last 10,000 races shows the following return:

Bets	Winners (%)	Average Return/£1
10,000	1108 (11.1)	-0.30

Therefore, on average, applying no skill to your horse selection would result in a loss of approximately 30p per £1 staked, betting at starting price. Add to this the cost of off-course betting tax (9%) and you would show a loss in the region of 40p per £1 staked.

This does, though, compare favourably with the National Lottery. The average loss per £1 staked on the National Lottery is an incredible 50p, although this includes tax. According to Tony Drapkin and Richard Forsyth, authors of *The Punter's Revenge*, a book I recommend for anyone interested in betting, especially those with access to a computer, the average loss for football pools is a staggering 73p per £1 staked. So we are obviously targeting the best option by concentrating on horseracing although it should be remembered that both Premium Bonds and the stock market offer a positive return per £1 invested, even if you select your share portfolio with no prior knowledge of the companies.

Calculating the return based on a random selection is not as pointless as it at first may seem. Since the starting price of the horse reflects the animal's chances to a reasonable degree of accuracy, the average return based on a random selection is a fair measure of the likely return against which to compare other selection methods. In other words, it shows how far the odds are stacked against the punter.

But how far *does* the starting price reflect the true chances of success? By converting the starting price to a probability it is possible to estimate how many winners would be expected over a period of time for each starting price category. The following table compares the actual number of winners against the expected number within each starting price band for approximately 200,000 race performances.

Table 1: Expected Number of Winners by Starting Price

Starting Price	Number Of Runners	Number Of Winners	Expected† Number Of Winners
Odds On	2718	1610	1647
Evens-2/1	8353	3104	3213
85/40-5/1	32081	6259	6740
11/2-10/1	50587	4928	5729
11/1-20/1	57162	2330	3475
22/1-40/1	31452	408	1013
50/1+	13756	53	218

† the expected number of winners is calculated from the starting price, therefore if the starting price exactly reflected the probability of success, the two right-most columns of the table would be equal.

The fact that the figures in the *expected* column always exceed the equivalent values in the Number Of Winners column is to be expected; this simply reflects the bookmakers margin. If a pair of the figures were similar it could be concluded that, for this particular price band, the odds accurately represent the probability of success.

The most interesting feature of the table is that the two *winners* columns diverge significantly as the starting price increases. For the odds on category, the difference is only minor, the actual number of winners equates to 98% of the expected number. However for the 22/1-40/1 price band the actual number of winners only amounts to 40% of those expected, and for the highest price band the percentage is just 24%. This illustrates one key fact: taken over a season as a whole, the higher priced horses represent poorer value. This can be further demonstrated by expanding the table of random selections.

Table 2: Average Return by Starting Price

Starting Price	Number Of Bets	Number Of Winners	Average Return/£1
Odds On	460	269	-0.08
Evens-2/1	1125	417	-0.06
85/40-5/1	3665	674	-0.17
11/2-10/1	4652	439	-0.21
11/1-20/1	4537	183	-0.36
22/1-40/1	2531	31	-0.64
50/1+	1171	11	-0.45
Total	**18141**	**2024**	**-0.30**

From Table 2 it can be seen that, on average, the higher priced horses (e.g. 11/1 and over) are very much under priced. Simply by modifying our random selection method to only pick horses that start at 10/1 or less reduces our loss per £1 bet from 30p to 18p. This bias in the starting price is an important facet of betting on Flat racing and is an issue we will return to in later sections.

In this section I have tried to illustrate how the odds are stacked in favour of the bookmaker, and to show that whilst some bets may appear more attractive (i.e. a 33/1 shot) they are, in fact, offering a poor rate of return when compared with the likely chance of success.

In the following section we concentrate on selection methods for two-year-old horses, and the factors that should be considered before placing a bet.

JUVENILES

Background Data

The previous section examined the relationship between the starting price and the likely success rate, and established that the price provides an accurate guide to the probability of a win but the higher prices substantially over estimate the probability. This trend also holds true for two-year-old horses, except that the poor value offered by the higher priced horses is accentuated. Table 3 illustrates this pattern:

Table 3: Average Return by Starting Price and Number of Runners

Starting Price		Number Of Runners 2-4	5-9	10-15	16+	All
Odds on	W	119	329	129	18	595
	R	185	526	221	33	965
	Ret	-0.01	0.03	-0.03	-0.08	0.00
Evens-2/1	W	96	497	294	70	957
	R	279	1346	762	192	2579
	Ret	-0.15	-0.06	-0.02	-0.09	-0.06
85/40-5/1	W	74	712	600	182	1568
	R	315	3507	2918	848	7588
	Ret	-0.02	-0.10	-0.06	-0.01	-0.07
11/2-10/1	W	22	303	443	183	951
	R	172	3378	4761	2097	10408
	Ret	0.11	-0.25	-0.21	-0.24	-0.22
11/1-20/1	W	3	136	188	140	467
	R	119	3066	5981	3931	13097
	Ret	-0.66	-0.30	-0.51	-0.44	-0.44
22/1-40/1	W	0	28	45	30	103
	R	47	1699	4151	3102	8999
	Ret	-1.00	-0.50	-0.67	-0.73	-0.66

(Table 3 continued)

50/1+	W	0	3	6	3	12
	R	18	779	1737	1479	4013
	Ret	-1.00	-0.80	-0.81	-0.90	-0.84
Total	**W**	**314**	**2008**	**1705**	**626**	**4653**
	R	**1135**	**14301**	**20531**	**11682**	**47649**
	Ret	**-0.15**	**-0.26**	**-0.41**	**-0.50**	**-0.38**

In the above table, *W* indicates the number of winners, *R* the number of runners and *Ret* the average return per £1 staked.

The loss per £1 staked for all two-year-olds is 38p, which exceeds the figure calculated for horses of any age (see previous section), and when the off-course tax liability is added the total loss per bet is nearing that of the National Lottery.

Again, the price of horses with a low probability of success, namely those priced at 20/1 or more, is greatly under stated. The most likely explanation for this fact is that two-year-olds are largely unexposed given that many will be making their racecourse debut and those with racing experience will not have raced many times. Consequently, bookmakers err on the side of caution and price the animals very conservatively. Interestingly, this feature seems to be independent of the number of runners in the race with the huge loss continued across all different runner categories. Given that the starting price offers such poor value for these low probability horses, does the Tote offer a better alternative? The following table is the result of analysing over 7,500 race performances for horses starting at more than 20/1 and comparing the starting price return with the Tote win return:

Bets	**Average SP Return/£1**	**Average Tote Return/£1**
7,565	-0.71	-0.56

Clearly, the Tote offers a better rate of return, but hardly enough to inspire a punter searching for a value bet.

Future Champions?

On the positive side though, the lower priced horses (i.e. horses priced up to 5/1) show a better rate of return than in the all-age analysis (-0.06 compared to -0.14) and the odds on shots show no loss at all. This trend is continued for juveniles making their first ever racecourse appearance which implies that the ability of the better two-year-old horses is known before they race. In other words, *stable talk* regarding the ability of the better two-year-old horses should not be dismissed out of hand.

To support this further, an analysis of 35 three-year-old Group I winners shows that 46% started favourite on their first run at two, and 60% started at less than 11/2. Furthermore, 71% finished in the first three on their racecourse debuts with 46% winning. All very interesting, but how does this help us to make money? Well, given that we are confidently able to identify horses with winning potential from their first run, it should be possible to turn this into profit.

Juveniles which win on their first run are not considered further, it is those which we know to be good animals but are beaten first time out which are most interesting. Of 72 two-year-old horses that started at evens or less on their racecourse debut and were beaten in the period 1989-94, 32 won on their next run giving an average profit of 0.41. Of the 40 horses which failed to win on their second run, 25 ran a third time with 10 winning, showing a profit of 0.31. Finally, of the 15 horses yet to win, 11 ran a fourth time with 3 winning, profit 0.15. Therefore, the following selection method should be borne in mind when considering two-year-old horses:

consider backing any two-year-old horse, which was beaten at evens or less on its debut, until it wins or has raced a further three times: expected profit 36p per £1 staked.

This theory can be extended further by introducing a date component. Since the better horses tend to make their debuts later in the year, it seems sensible to restrict the analysis to the period June to October. The following results were generated by considering all beaten first time out two-year-old favourites on their next racecourse outing, within the period June to October: 108 winners from 349 bets, profit 0.24. Whilst this is less than the 36p per £1 achieved previously, it is significantly higher than the expected 38p loss and greater than the percentage most professional gamblers hope to achieve. Therefore,

> *consider backing any two-year-old horse from June to October, which was a beaten favourite (or joint favourite) on its debut, on its next run: expected profit 24p per £1 staked.*

This selection technique can be further refined by considering the type of track on which the horse made its debut. The more prestigious courses seem to produce higher returns from their debutantes. For instance, restricting the above procedure to include only horses making their debuts at Ascot, Goodwood, Kempton, Newmarket, and York improves the return to 53p per £1 staked from 88 bets over the period 1989-94. Therefore,

> *consider backing any two-year-old horse which was a beaten favourite (or joint favourite) on its debut at either Ascot, Goodwood, Kempton, Newmarket or York on its next run: expected profit 53p per £1 staked.*

Form Analysis

We have seen that winning form is not necessarily the most critical variable when looking for ways to make a profit. The following table shows the win rate and average return for juveniles categorised by their most recent racecourse performance:

Table 4: Average Return and Strike Rate by Distance Beaten on Latest Start

Distance Beaten Last Time†	Winners	(%)	Runners	Average Return/£1
0	711	(19.2)	3703	-0.22
0.01-0.1	46	(20.2)	228	-0.27
0.11-1.0	405	(22.5)	1803	-0.12
1.01-2.0	316	(18.6)	1695	-0.20
2.01-3.0	331	(17.6)	1879	-0.19
3.01-4.0	272	(15.0)	1819	-0.21
4.01-5.0	234	(13.3)	1760	-0.27
5.01-10.0	796	(9.7)	8191	-0.28
10.01-20.0	500	(5.0)	9947	-0.50
20+ lengths	135	(3.2)	4280	-0.59
All	**3746**	**(10.6)**	**35305**	**-0.35**

† distance beaten last time is given in horse lengths.

There is not a great deal to help us in Table 4, however it is interesting to see how the percentage of winners to runners declines as the distance beaten last time increases. The strike rate for horses beaten up to one length last time is just over 20%, whereas for those beaten over 5 lengths it is only a little over 6%. However, this poorer strike rate isn't fully reflected in the starting price as demonstrated by the declining average return, to a loss of 59p per £1.

Table 5: Average Return by Distance Beaten and Starting Price on Latest Start

Distance Beaten Last Time†		Starting Price Last Time: Odds On	Ev-5/1	11/2-20/1	22/1+	All
0	W	127	401	173	10	711
	R	482	2001	1128	92	3703
	Ret	-0.14	-0.22	-0.23	-0.30	-0.22
0.01-2.0	W	35	392	307	33	767
	R	145	1593	1745	243	3726
	Ret	-0.35	-0.06	-0.22	-0.38	-0.16
2.01-5.0	W	10	341	423	63	837
	R	68	1726	3032	632	5458
	Ret	-0.46	-0.13	-0.22	-0.46	-0.22
5.01-10.0	W	14	218	455	109	796
	R	53	1440	4875	1823	8191
	Ret	0.54	-0.05	-0.30	-0.41	-0.28
10.01-20	W	4	90	289	117	500
	R	16	862	5070	3999	9947
	Ret	0.01	-0.27	-0.44	-0.61	-0.50
20+ lgths	W	4	27	74	30	135
	R	4	187	1672	5417	4280
	Ret	1.43	-0.13	-0.43	-0.73	-0.59
Total	**W**	**194**	**1469**	**1721**	**362**	**3746**
	R	**768**	**7809**	**17522**	**9206**	**35305**
	Ret	**-0.15**	**-0.14**	**-0.33**	**-0.58**	**-0.35**

† distance beaten last time is given in horse lengths. In the above table, *W* indicates the number of winners, *R* the number of runners and *Ret* the average return per £1 staked.

Table 5 above shows that although horses beaten a long way last time out show a poor return in general, a better determining factor to their potential profitability is the price at which they started. This ties in with our earlier findings relating to first time out favourites and shows that horses should not be excluded from calculations simply because they performed poorly on their most recent run. Starting at a short price for their last race indicates a certain level of perceived ability (or potential) and therefore they should not be discounted due to one poor run, especially since their price is possibly now over stated. Therefore,

> *consider backing any two-year-old horse that was beaten more than five lengths last time and started at odds on: expected profit 47p per £1 staked.*

This theory runs counter to conventional race analysis arguments which tend to prefer animals with good recent form. It is purely this fact that makes the well beaten short priced horse a good bet on its next run.

This selection method also demonstrates the difference between looking for runners which are expected to provide a profitable long term return and merely backing the animals which appear most likely to win.

Nurseries and the Time Factor

Handicaps for two-year-old horses are notoriously difficult to evaluate. Normally, they are contested by large fields of unexposed, probably improving, animals with the added problem of the weight differences introduced by the BHB Handicappers. You may have guessed that this is not a type of race with which I am particularly enamoured. However, there is a way of generating a profit from a small number of bets each season, but firstly we need to consider some general points about nurseries.

In essence, a two-year-old may run in a nursery if it has been allotted a handicap mark by the BHB. Before it can be handicapped it must either have won at least once in two starts or have raced three times. Therefore, horses can appear in nurseries after finishing well beaten in non-handicap events and thus be almost impossible to handicap, especially if they have been *tenderly handled* and have only really been racing to gain experience. How can an accurate assessment be made of a horse which has finished mid-division in three large fields, not finishing within 10 lengths of the winner?

Notwithstanding the problems associated with this race type, winners can be found by closely studying race times. Alex Bird commented that any two-year-old which produces a race time which is faster than older horses over the same distance on the same track on the same day must have above average ability. This is the principle we can use.

Analysing all juveniles which qualify under the above criterion for the 1992-94 Flat racing seasons produced the following results: backing the selected juveniles until they win or have raced a further three times produced 10 winners from 66 bets, with a profit of 0.37. Therefore,

> *consider backing any two-year-old horse, which won or was beaten less than 1 length in a nursery in a time better than the older horses over the same distance on the same track on the same day, until it wins or has raced a further three times: expected profit 37p per £1 staked.*

This selection procedure is based on a sound theoretical approach, unfortunately there are very few bets each year, and at 15% the winners to runners strike rate is on the low side.

Calculating Speed Figures for Juveniles

In general, race times can be very informative for two-year-old horses. It is possible to extend the above approach to generate ratings for the majority of juvenile runners. Speed ratings can be calculated by combining the race time achieved by the two-year-old, the weight it carried, a race time produced by an older horse in a handicap over the same distance at the course, the weight it carried and the BHB handicap mark for the older horse. The rating can be calculated as follows:

1. Subtract the time (in seconds) produced by the 2-y.o from that produced by the older horse and multiply by 18.
2. Add the weight carried (in pounds) by the 2-y.o and subtract the weight carried by the older horse.
3. Add the BHB handicap rating for the older horse.
4. If the older horse is 4 years or older, add the weight allowance 3-y.o's receive from older horses.
5. If the 2-y.o was beaten, multiply the distance beaten by 15 and divide by the distance of the race (in furlongs) and subtract this from the total.

Given further explanation it is quite easy to see how the above formula works. Step 1 converts the time difference between the two races into pounds, the standard unit for expressing ability. The 18 is simply derived from the average number of lengths a two-year-old horse travels per second, 6, multiplied by the weight allowed per length, normally 3lbs. (The weight allowance per length varies as the race distance varies and is best determined by dividing the race distance in furlongs into 15, so for 5f races the value is 3lbs, and for 10 furlong races the value is 1½lbs. Therefore, this routine could be improved, but further complicated, by using 6 multiplied by 15 divided by the race distance instead of the 18). Step 2 adjusts for the difference in weight carried by the horses. Step 3 introduces the BHB handicap rating, the basis for the time rating. The fourth step adjusts for the maturity of the older horse, to allow 2-y.o's to be compared with horses of any age. The final step simply uses the procedure outlined above to reduce the rating for beaten two-year-old horses.

This routine produces reasonable time ratings, but it is important to ensure that the two comparison races are directly comparable, namely over the course and distance and that the non-juvenile race is a handicap. In strict terms only races taking place on the same day should be used. However, if a comparable race is not available, it is possible to compare with a race staged either the day before or the day after, providing the ground conditions have not changed significantly. Use the race times to determine whether the going has changed, don't rely on the BHB going reports which leave a great deal to be desired in terms of accuracy.

Speed Figure Calculation - Example 1

Alhaarth, a two-year-old trained by Major Hern made his debut on the July course at Newmarket on 11 July 1995. He started favourite at 7/2 in a 16 runner 7 furlong maiden, and won carrying 9st in a time of 1m 26.32s, 1.96 seconds slower than the standard time. On the same day, Bouche Bee, a three-year-old trained by L Cumani won a 7 furlong class B handicap on the same course, carrying 8st 3lbs and taking 1m 27.06s, 2.66 seconds slower than the standard time. Bouche Bee was rated 87 at the time by the BHB. To calculate Alhaarth's speed figure for the race:

Step 1 *Find the difference in the times and multiply by 18.*

87.06 - 86.32	=	0.74
0.74 x 18	=	13.32

Step 2 *Add weight carried by 2yo, subtract weight carried by older horse.*

13.32 + 126 - 115	=	24.32

Step 3 *Add BHB handicap rating for the older horse.*

24.32 + 87	=	111.32

Step 4 *Not applicable for these races.*

Step 5 *Not applicable for this horse.*

Final rating **111**.

Speed Figure Calculation - Example 2

Dark Deed, a two-year-old filly trained by B Hills made her racecourse debut at Newbury over 6 furlongs on 11 August 1995. She carried 8st 11lbs and was beaten 3¾ lengths by Bosra Sham who recorded a time of 1m 13.87s, 2.07 seconds slower than the standard time. On the same card, Great Hall, a six year old trained by P Cundell won the 6 furlong sprint carrying 7st 5lbs in a time of 1m 13.61s, 1.81 seconds slower than the standard time. Great Hall was rated 57 by the BHB at the time. To calculate Dark Deed's speed rating:

Step 1 *Find the difference in the times and multiply by 18.*

73.61 - 73.87	=	-0.26
-0.26 x 18	=	-4.68

Step 2 *Add weight carried by 2yo, subtract weight carried by older horse.*

-4.68 + 123 - 103	=	15.32

Step 3 *Add BHB handicap rating for the older horse.*

15.32 + 57	=	72.32

Step 4 *Adjust for weight-for-age.*

72.32 + 5	=	77.32

Step 5 *Adjust for the distance beaten.*

77.32 - (3.75x15÷6)	=	67.95

Final rating **68**.

It is important to note that the ratings calculated using the above procedure are not directly comparable, in absolute terms, to ratings published by other organisations, i.e. *Raceform*, Timeform and BHB. For instance, the BHB rating for Dark Deed may be vastly different from the 68 we have calculated, however this would be due, in part, to a difference in scale. The BHB, and other organisations, use a fixed scale to allow the comparison of juvenile ratings with ratings for older horses, and to compare with animals from other countries. We are simply using the ratings to indicate the relative merits of the two-year-old horses running in a particular season and therefore can use any scale we choose. For example, we could add 20 lbs to each rating and not change their meaning, since the difference between the ratings of two horses would remain the same. For example, no matter how we change the scale, Alhaarth will always be 43 lbs superior to Dark Deed based on just these two runs alone.

The main advantage with these approaches is that they both side-step the inherent problems of race time analysis, namely differences in racecourse configuration and variability of ground conditions. When comparing times from different race courses it is necessary to adjust each time for type of track and going. Some courses place little emphasis on stamina, such as Epsom where the 5f course is mainly downhill, which enables horses to complete the course in approximately 55 seconds. In contrast, the sprint course at Beverley is extremely stiff with horses taking about 62 seconds to complete an equivalent distance.

The differences in going are even harder to handle. The going is not measured at all accurately in this country, and the only way to assess the speed of the track is to examine the race times after racing. (See the non-juvenile section for a discussion on the going allowance.)

Since the above procedures only compare horses running on the same track on the same day, the state of the ground and the stiffness of the course can be safely ignored (unless there is sufficient rain during the afternoon to change the ground), simplifying the calculations considerably.

Using Speed Figures

Once calculated the juvenile speed figures can be used in three different ways. Firstly, there is the conventional approach of taking a speed rating for each horse in a race, adjusting for the weight carried, and using the resultant figures as a guide to the chances of each horse. As an example, we will take the Stamford Bridge Conditions Stakes run at York on the 7 October 1995. The runners with their respective weights, speed figures and adjusted speed figures are given below.

Table 6: Adjusted Speed Figures for the Stamford Bridge Conditions Stakes

Horse	Weight (lbs)	Raw Speed Figure	Adjusted Speed Figure
Tria Kemata	9-0 (126)	54	54
Sualtach	8-12 (124)	41	43
Believe Me	8-9 (121)	70	75
Bullfinch	8-9 (121)	44	49

From the ratings (the best each horse has achieved in its last three runs), this looks any easy race for Believe Me. However, although Believe Me won at odds of 9/2 it was only by a neck from Bullfinch (5/2), with a further ½ length back to the even money favourite Tria Kemata. Sualtach was virtually pulled up in fourth. Interestingly, the first three had met on their last start with Tria Kemata winning the race with about 3½ lengths to spare over Believe Me in fifth, and Bullfinch a further 2½ back in sixth. This explains why Tria Kemata started a short priced favourite. I ought to point out here that I do **not** use the speed figures in this conventional fashion, I tend to prefer the following two options.

The second way of utilising the speed figures concerns ante-post betting. It is possible to highlight exceptional two-year-old horses just from speed figures. If the horse records a good relative time early on in its career it may be possible to secure a big price ante-post for one of the following year's classics, safe in the knowledge that the animal is well above average ability. Using a purely form based guide it is almost impossible to place an ante-post bet at reasonable odds, since as soon as the horse races against, and beats the higher rated horses, its ante-post price is reduced before a bet is possible. Ante-post prices are not just contracted due to weight of money, if a two-year-old horse produces an impressive performance its price is reduced immediately, before further money is taken.

The third, and in my opinion most valuable, facet of the speed figures concerns rating *races* as opposed to horses. If a winner records a particularly good figure it is worth noting those horses which finished behind it. In this case, the speed figure is used as a guide to the quality of the race. For instance, when Alhaarth recorded the 111 on 11 July, it was by far the best juvenile rating recorded by that stage of the 1995 season. This indicated that the race was of above average quality and that the runners who finished within a reasonable distance of Alhaarth were worth following. In fact, of the 16 runners, 9 went on to win at least one race, and four out of the first five (those within seven lengths of the winner) won subsequent races.

The advantage of following animals of this type is that the form is initially hard to assess since, in all probability, very few of the horses will have run before. This absence of form lines provides the ideal situation for the speed figure punter who is in possession of the only reliable guide to the quality of the race.

Summary

Juveniles provide a good source of profit, especially those which are highly regarded but fail early on in their careers. The higher priced runners should be avoided unless they have previously raced at much shorter odds showing that they are thought to have some potential, however well it may be hidden. Pay special regard to those animals well beaten at short prices at the more prestigious racecourses. Finally, avoid nursery races, unless a horse records a particularly good time compared to older animals, and make use of the speed figures in a way that best suits your style of betting.

NON-JUVENILES

Races for non-juveniles (i.e. those horses aged three years and upwards) make up the majority of all Flat races in Great Britain. They can be categorised into three classes: pattern races, Other non-handicaps and handicaps. *Pattern races* are the most prestigious races and are subdivided into Group 1, Group 2, Group 3 and Listed races. Group 1 events carry the most prize money, with all the *classics* carrying Group 1 status. For the purposes of continuity and comparison, Listed races could be thought of as Group 4 events since they carry the lowest prize money of all the pattern races. *Other non-handicaps* is a term used to refer to all non pattern races in which horses are not allotted weight by the BHB Handicappers relative to their abilities. Therefore, this grouping covers maidens, claimers, stakes races, selling races and some amateur, apprentice and Ladies races. *Handicaps* make up the remainder of races.

Pattern events are normally considered the most reliable race type for betting purposes simply because they are contested by the best animals. At the other end of the scale, poor quality selling races are often contested by the poorest horses in training, and those of dubious character and temperament, and the punter cannot be entirely sure whether his/her selection will actually make an effort to win. Handicap races on the Flat are very competitive, especially the sprints, and therefore are often the most difficult to assess.

The better Flat racehorses tend to stop racing after their three- or four-year-old seasons much to the disappointment of their supporters. Some animals, however, are campaigned for many seasons with a few still racing after they have reached double figures. The age of a horse is often overlooked by the punter when making a selection, but as the following table shows it is a variable that should be considered:

Table 7: Average Return and Strike Rate By Age of Horse

Age of Horse	Winners (%)	Runners	Average Return/£1
3	7360 (10.0)	73928	-0.34
4	3181 (8.9)	35548	-0.27
5	1767 (9.9)	17829	-0.19
6	923 (9.2)	10010	-0.25
7	428 (7.6)	5644	-0.38
8	236 (7.8)	3022	-0.44
9+	142 (5.7)	2480	-0.48
All	**14037 (9.5)**	**148461**	**-0.31**

Clearly, the younger horses have a better wins to runs strike rate, with seemingly a significant decrease in the percentage from ages six to seven years. A further drop in the strike rate occurs when the age of the horse exceeds eight years. This is reflected in the average return, with horses over eight years old returning a loss of 48p per £1 staked compared with an average loss of 31p per £1 for all horses. This means that the age factor is not considered by the bookmakers which makes these horses, in general, poorer value.

In the following sections we investigate ways of turning this 31p loss into a profit. Firstly, non-handicap races are considered, and special attention is paid to the use of race times to highlight future winners. Secondly, handicap races are analysed, and such factors as the draw, trainer, recent performances and previous race comments are examined.

NON-HANDICAPS

With no artificial handicapping of the runners, non-handicaps are, in general, less competitive than handicaps, and as a consequence should be easier to evaluate. Unfortunately, this reduced level of competition is reflected in the prices on offer by the bookmakers and so making a profit is still difficult. However, one of the best guides to potential winners that I have found is the race time.

Using Race Times

In the section on Juveniles, we looked at how race times could be used to identify probable future winners and generate time ratings. We also covered the problems associated with using race times, specifically the unreliable nature of the going assessments and the diversity in the racecourse configurations across the country. This latter problem is, to some extent, nullified by the introduction of a race standard time. Both the trade papers, as well as Timeform and *Raceform*, produce standard times for each race distance on every course in Great Britain. Such times are supposed to represent the likely time a horse rated 100 by the BHB would take to run the course on good to firm going. The use of these standards enables the comparison of race times produced by different horses on different tracks, however it does not take account of the varying ground conditions.

It was mentioned earlier that the difference in the going from course to course, or even day to day, is a more difficult problem to solve than that of racecourse configuration. In his book *Betting For A Living*, Nick Mordin recommends the calculation of a going allowance based on the races staged on the course on a particular day. This figure can then be used to normalise for the effect of the going at different courses. To determine the going allowance, Mordin suggests that the differences between the actual race times and the standard times are first divided by the race distances and then averaged after any freak figures have been removed.
Therefore, for a six race card, the times may have been:

Table 8: Calculation of Going Allowance

Race Dist.	Race Time (s)	Standard Time (s)	Diff. (s)	Diff. per Furlong
5	63.18	60.00	3.18	0.64
12	157.99	154.60	5.39	0.45
10	136.08	124.70	11.38	1.63

7	89.90	85.70	4.20	0.60
7	92.19	85.70	6.49	0.93
10	134.15	124.70	9.45	0.95

It could be argued that the time for the third race is an outlier and should be removed from the going allowance calculation. Consequently, the going allowance becomes the average of the other five times, namely 0.71 seconds per furlong. In fact, Nick Mordin generally takes the average of the three fastest times excluding any outliers, although there are no hard and fast rules governing the number of races you use. Special attention is required for courses with different tracks. For example, Kempton and Sandown each have a sprint track running through the centre of the course. Naturally, the going could vary considerably from the main course to the sprint track, a feature which would need to be accounted for in the going allowance.

Once the going allowance has been calculated it is possible to calculate a speed figure for any runner on the card. Firstly, it is necessary to adjust the time of the winner by the going allowance, to produce a normalised time. Therefore, if the going allowance indicates that the track is riding faster than the norm, the winning time is increased accordingly. For instance, if, in a 5 furlong sprint, the track is found to be riding 0.1 seconds per furlong faster than the standard, the time of the winner should be increased by 0.5 seconds (i.e. 5 x 0.1). This new time being an estimate of the time the horse would have recorded on average going.

To convert the time to a rating it is necessary to consider the standard race time for the distance. At this point, it is necessary to set the scale for the ratings. Normally, a horse producing a time equivalent to the standard would be given a rating of 100, before adjusting for weight carried. However, any figure could be used to determine the rating scale. The next step is to determine the difference between the standard time and the adjusted time, in seconds. This figure is multiplied by 6 (lengths run per second) and then further multiplied by the ratio of 15 to the race distance. The resultant figure is either added to, or subtracted from, 100 depending on whether the adjusted time is faster, or slower than the standard time. Finally, the figure should be adjusted for the weight carried and distance beaten by the winner. For a more detailed description of calculating speed figures see *Betting For A Living* by Nick Mordin.

Clearly, the power of the time analysis methods outlined in the juvenile section is derived from the fact that neither require the use of a standard time or going allowance, which are, after all, subject to their own degree of error.

The following method for selecting horses with winning potential utilises the race time and standard time but not the going allowance, which, due to its approximate method of calculation, is the component subject to the highest degree of error.

Only good horses win pattern races, and if they record a time faster than the standard it implies that the race was run at a true pace and that the form is worth following. Backing any non-juvenile winner, or runner-up which finished within ½ length of the winner, of a pattern race for which the time was faster than the standard, until it wins or competes in three further races, produced the following results from the three seasons 1992-94: 26 winners from 85 bets (31% strike rate) with a profit of 0.38. Therefore,

> *consider backing any non-juvenile winner, or runner-up finishing within ½ length of the winner, of a pattern race for which the time recorded was faster than the standard, until it wins or has raced a further three times: expected profit 38p per £1 staked.*

Naturally, whether a race is run in a time below the standard is very much dependent on the going. The qualifying performances for the 85 bets discussed above were all run on good or faster ground. Obviously, if we experience a wet summer there will be very few bets due to the softened state of the ground which is not particularly helpful if you are relying on these bets to provide an income.

Fortunately it is possible to extend the scope of this method by changing the way we use the race times. Rather than just using the races with times faster than the standard, the following method uses the best time of the day. The best time of the day is simply the fastest time relative to the standards. For example, given the six races:

Race Number	Difference from Standard Time
1	+1.8
2	+3.0
3	+2.9
4	+6.2
5	+3.9
6	+2.0

The best race time of the day was recorded in race 1 since this time is closest to the standard and all race times exceeded their comparable standards. In the next example, the best race time was recorded in race 4, the race which produced a time 4.9 seconds faster than the standard (hence the minus sign). The next best time of the day would be race 1 at 0.1 seconds under the standard.

Race Number	Difference from Standard Time
1	-0.1
2	+3.5
3	+2.6
4	-4.9
5	+9.9
6	+1.0

For this selection procedure only one horse can qualify from any one meeting in a day. However, from the above example it can be seen that it is possible for two or more horses to qualify under the previous selection routine.

Backing any non-juvenile winner, or runner-up which finished within ½ length of the winner, of a Group race which produced the best time of the day until it wins or has run a further three times, produced the following results for the three seasons 1992 to 1994: 27 winners from 116 (23% strike rate) with a profit of 0.87. Therefore,

> *consider backing any non-juvenile winner, or runner-up finishing within ½ length of the winner, of a Group race which had the best time of the day, until it wins or has raced a further three times: expected profit 87p per £1 staked.*

Although race times are difficult to interpret given the problems mentioned above, they do provide a good indicator of the likely future success of a pattern race winner, or runner-up. To generate the results given above I have used the standard times published by *Raceform*, and whilst I would not advise readers against using other standard times, I would certainly recommend checking the methods outlined for a season or two (historically) to make sure the different times do not have any hidden discrepancies.

Normally, one would expect time based procedures such as these to only produce qualifying horses from the longer distance races, since it should be easier to produce a faster relative time, in absolute terms, in a long distance race than in a sprint. However, the qualifying performances for 1992-94 are fairly well distributed over all races distances with only 20% of the horses qualifying in sprint races. Had this distribution been strongly biased towards one end of the race distance scale it would have been necessary to consider the ratio of the time difference from the standard to the actual race distance. Fortunately, this is not required and the simpler approaches outlined previously seem to work well.

Favourites

Some of the selection procedures we have discussed so far have relatively low wins to bets strike rates which increases the possibility of long losing runs. This can have a detrimental effect on the way we bet and result in missing good priced winners due to our natural reluctance to continue a losing sequence. Having an additional approach with a high strike rate helps to break up the long losing runs and restore confidence, and here the favourites come in.

In *Value Betting*, Mark Coton suggests that, whilst it is dangerous to make generalisations in betting, favourites are, by definition, bad value. This is true to a certain extent, however it is possible to find some favourites which are worth supporting. These bets tend to be at either end of the race distance scale, namely, 5 furlongs and 15 furlongs plus, and in small fields. All non-handicaps were analysed for the period 1990-94 and the following results obtained. Backing all clear favourites in 5 furlong non-handicaps in fields of 2 to 4 runners would have resulted in 30 bets and 21 winners, a strike rate of 70% and a profit of 0.22. Therefore,

> *consider backing all clear favourites in 5 furlong non-handicap races in fields of 2 to 4 runners: expected profit 22p per £1 staked.*

At the other end of the distance scale, and over the same period of analysis, backing all clear favourites in non-handicaps of 15 furlongs or more in fields of 2 to 4 runners would have resulted in 26 bets and 21 winners, a strike rate of 81% with a profit of 0.27. Therefore,

> *consider backing all clear favourites in non-handicaps over 15 furlongs or more in fields of 2 to 4 runners: expected profit 27p per £1 staked.*

With such a high strike rate the average price of these runners is going to be low, but any long term profit should always be welcomed.

HANDICAPS

Any punter who spends hours analysing a big field of Flat handicappers in the hope of finding the winner either has time to kill or enjoys a challenge. Handicaps are notoriously difficult to evaluate, and it is interesting to note that the majority of races sponsored by bookmakers are handicaps, for obvious reasons. However, the property that makes this type of race such a challenge (i.e. the normalising effect of the different weights carried) also has the effect of introducing a degree of uniformity across the race grade, which is advantageous to anyone using a systematic approach to betting.

There is, sometimes, an element of confusion concerning the relationship between handicap ratings and weight carried. A handicap mark is simply a convenient way of expressing the ability of one horse relative to another. For example, if two three-year-old colts were rated 87 and 97, the latter could be said to be 10 pounds superior to the former and in a handicap race would carry 10 pounds more weight. The ratings do not determine the amount of weight to be carried, just the weight one horse will carry relative to another. Therefore, it would be possible for these two horses to be set to carry 7-10 and 8-06 in one race, and 8-11 and 9-07 in another race on the same day. The absolute weight carried is determined by the rating of the highest rated horse in the race. In these two hypothetical races, the top rated horse in the first race would be rated higher than the top rated horse in the second race, by eleven pounds, in fact.

This is an important distinction to make, and it is imperative to remember that a horse carrying 9-07, for instance, is not necessarily badly handicapped, and an animal set to carry

7-07 is not guaranteed to be well handicapped. The weight carried by a horse simply reflects the overall strength of the race. Just because a Flat handicapper is set to carry 10-0 is no reason to assume it cannot win.

Trainer Effect

A question that has arisen recently is whether horses trained by the *top* trainers in the country are handicapped purely on their racecourse performances or placed higher in the handicap simply due to the trainers' above average strike rates. This type of query can be tested easily using races over several seasons.

Due to the uniformity of handicaps, it is a simple task to work out how many wins each stable should have relative to the number of horses run and the size of the fields in which they compete. It is then possible to compare the expected number of winners against the actual number of successes. If the trainers' hypothesis is correct the top trainers will have fewer actual winners than expected.

The following table summarises the actual and expected number of winners for sixteen trainers based on races run over several seasons:

Table 9: Expected Compared to Actual Number of Non-Juvenile Handicap Winners by Trainer

Trainer	Number of Rns	Number of Wins	%	Expected Number of Wins
R Akehurst	1265	182	14.4	111
J L Dunlop	1055	174	16.5	104
J H M Gosden	647	114	17.6	57
Sir Mark Prescott	645	117	18.1	62
M Johnston	1210	162	13.4	115
I A Balding	965	130	13.5	89
Mrs M Reveley	502	87	17.3	51

Lord Huntingdon	575	82	14.3	49
L M Cumani	524	79	15.1	48
B W Hills	783	103	13.2	72
G Harwood	675	91	13.5	62
J Berry	1359	155	11.4	127
Mrs J R Ramsden	1051	115	10.9	87
M R Stoute	734	98	13.4	71
H R A Cecil	339	61	18.0	36
A C Stewart	350	56	16.0	31

The trainers listed above each have had more winners than expected, with Reg Akehurst exceeding the number of expected winners by 71, 64%. This seems to imply that, in general, none of the trainers listed in the table have any reason to complain, although it is possible that individual horses are badly handicapped from time to time. It could be argued that these trainers only run their better handicapped horses in handicap races, keeping their poorly handicapped animals to non-handicap events. Personally, though, I would prefer to back a handicapper trained by someone whose actual number of winners exceeds the number expected whether they believe the Handicapper treats them fairly or not.
Interestingly, of trainers listed in Table 9, only three show an overall profit from betting on all of their handicap runners, namely, R Akehurst, J Gosden and G Harwood.

The following list includes all trainers who have a recorded at least 20% more winners than expected, during the period of analysis, and have had 10 or more handicap winners in total:

R Akehurst
D W P Arbuthnot
R W Armstrong
I A Balding
R Bastiman
J Berry
M J Camacho
H R A Cecil
R Charlton
B Hanbury
P W Harris
G Harwood
P C Haslam
Major W R Hern
Lady Herries
A Hide
C J Hill
B W Hills
D R Loder
P J Makin
D Morley
D Murray-Smith
R J O'Sullivan
J Pearce
M C Pipe
Sir Mark Prescott
Mrs J R Ramsden

P F I Cole	Lord Huntingdon	Mrs M Reveley
L M Cumani	R Ingram	M J Ryan
P D Cundell	M A Jarvis	A C Stewart
C A Cyzer	W Jarvis	M R Stoute
J L Dunlop	M Johnston	H Thomson-Jones
D R C Elsworth	Bob Jones	P T Walwyn
P S Felgate	S E Kettlewell	J W Watts
J H M Gosden	G Lewis	G Wragg

Clues From Previous Races

Due to the uniformity of handicaps, we may be able to derive some useful clues as to the likely chance of success of a horse from previous races. In theory, if a horse had a good chance of winning one handicap, providing the conditions have not changed radically, i.e. different race distance, a change to the going or a marked increase in the animal's handicap mark, it should have a relatively similar chance in another handicap. At first sight this assumption looks rather dubious, however it can be supported with the following evidence.

We have seen that it is possible to estimate the probability that a horse will win based on its starting price. If we assume the above theory to be correct, then the chance of a horse winning a handicap could be determined by the chance it had of winning its *latest handicap*. Table 10, based on almost 70,000 race performances, illustrates this idea :

Table 10: Average Return and Strike Rate by Price in Previous Handicap Race

Starting Price in previous Handicap	Winners	(%)	Runners	Average Return/£1
Odds On	50	(22.2)	489	-0.08
Evens-5/1	1957	(14.2)	13761	-0.15
11/2-20/1	3983	(9.0)	44026	-0.22

22/1+	438	(4.4)	9917	-0.45
All	**6428**	**(9.5)**	**67929**	**-0.24**

Therefore, of the 489 runners who started at odds on for their latest race (a handicap), 50 won their next handicap, a strike rate of 22.2%, which is more than double the strike rate for all runners.

Interestingly, horses which ran most recently in a pattern race return a loss of 38p per £1 staked if running next in a handicap. If their previous race was a non-handicap outside the pattern classification the loss increases to 39p per £1 staked. These poor returns compare to a loss of only 24p per £1 staked if the horse ran in a handicap most recently.

The poor returns associated with horses running in non-handicap events prior to a handicap is due to a combination of under pricing and cautious handicapping. Horses stepping down in class from pattern races to handicaps are often poorly priced simply due to this change in race status. However, it is often overlooked that the reason for the drop in class is that they do not have the necessary ability to compete at the higher levels. Frequently, horses run in claiming or selling races after a number of fruitless runs in handicaps. Unfortunately, if they run well, or even win, one of these races they will be re-handicapped and possibly raised in the weights. Therefore, their chance of winning, when returning to handicaps, is poorer than it was before they ventured into non-handicap company, and, to make matters worse, their starting price will often be lower in relative terms simply because they have *good,* or *winning,* recent form. Clearly, these are horses to avoid.

Even without imposing restrictions on the race distance etc. it can be seen from the Table 10 that, for handicap races, the chance of success can be estimated from the starting price of the horse in its most recent handicap. Both the average return and winners to runners strike rate decline as the price increases. This clearly demonstrates the uniform nature of this race type and the poor value offered about higher priced horses, which we covered earlier.

Although Table 10 provides useful information, it is not going to make us rich. In fact, all the figures in the average return column are negative meaning we will actually lose in the long run. The least-worst category, though, is the odds on group. So can we turn the 8p loss per £1 staked into a profit?

Another variable we need to consider when using the starting price in a previous race as a guide, is the number of runners raced against. Breaking down the odds on category by runners gives the following:

Table 11: Average Return and Strike Rate by Number of Runners in Previous Race for Horses which Started Odds On for their Latest Run in a Handicap

Number of runners in previous Handicap	Winners	(%)	Runners	Average Return/£1
2-4	9	(14.1)	64	-0.50
5-9	30	(23.6)	127	0.02
10-15	10	(31.3)	32	0.33
16+	1	(50.0)	2	0.63
All	**50**	**(22.2)**	**225**	**-0.08**

As the number of runners in the previous race increases, so does the strike rate and average return in the next race. The reason for this is that a horse starting at odds on in a 2-4 runner handicap is nothing out of the ordinary, but one starting at odds on in a larger field, say 14 runners, is clearly thought to be a *good thing* by the betting public. The animal is probably ideally suited by the race conditions, is very well handicapped (i.e. on a low handicapped mark) and

is possibly improving. This is just the type of horse we want to have a bet on; but not in this race. All the factors which make it a good thing have been accounted for by the price, after all it is odds on and therefore, does not offer anything in the way of value. It is on its next run when we can start to think about a bet.
The price of the odds on shot will, in all probability, be higher next time it runs. This could be due to a number of factors. Firstly, if the horse won when odds on, it will have been pushed up the weights by the Handicapper (or carrying a penalty), and thus appear less attractive. Secondly, if it was well beaten, the lack of *good recent form* will lead to an increase in the starting price. Thirdly, the reason it started odds on may have been due to the perceived lack of quality opposition, which may not be the case on its next run. However, the fact that it was considered to be a good thing for its last handicap remains, and this, combined with our belief of a high degree of uniformity amongst handicap races, makes this horse a value option on its next run. Table 11 above supports this theory. Unfortunately, there are only a few bets of this type each year.

It is possible, though, to extend the coverage of the *odds on* approach simply by considering the two most recent races as opposed to just the latest race. By backing any handicapper, which, in either of its last two handicap races, started at odds on in fields of 10 runners or more would produce the following results: 28 winners from 91 bets, a strike rate of 31% with a profit of 0.37. Therefore,

> *consider backing any handicap runner which, in either of its last two handicap races started at odds on in a field of 10 runners or more: expected profit 37p per £1 staked.*

How about horses which did not start at odds on in their latest handicap, can we make a profit from these?

Firstly, we need to divide these horses into two groups: those which won their last race and those which were beaten. Secondly, we need to examine the way in which they run. The best data available regarding the style of running are the comments-in-running. Such comments are printed in the results section of *Raceform, the Official Formbook* and Racing Post. It may also be possible to discern this required information from other publications, such as Timeform and the Sporting Life. The comments give the reader an invaluable insight into the running of the race, including where the horse was positioned at different stages, whether it was hampered at a crucial point and how well it finished.

Considering the winners group first, it would seem logical to select horses to follow which won their latest race very easily. The race comments to look for would include: *easily, comfortable, canter* and *unchallenged.* However, by doing this we are adopting a more conventional approach to race analysis which is precisely what this book is trying to show will only lead to losing. In fact, if we did back all the handicappers which won their last handicap at odds against and received the comment: *easily, very easily, canter, comfortably, readily, unchallenged* or *cleverly,* we would back only 71 winners from 336 bets in the period 1990-94, a strike rate of 21% with a loss of 18p per £1 staked.

Surprisingly, this loss of 18p per £1 staked is worse than the loss incurred by randomly selecting horses, which won their previous handicap at odds against (i.e. 12p loss per £1 staked). This indicates the level of under pricing associated with this type of handicap runner.

So, the obvious selection will not necessarily yield a profit. An alternative winner to follow is one which *quickens* at the end of a race. A horse which exhibits this quality is harder for the Handicapper to assess and is often not penalised sufficiently. Backing all horses running in a handicap which had won their previous handicap at odds against and received the comment *quickened* would have produced the following results: 92 winners from 421 bets, a strike rate of 22% with a profit of 0.13.

For the losing group it is necessary to concentrate on horses which only just failed to win their last race. Therefore, acceptable comments are: *just failed, caught close home* and *caught post*. Backing all horses in handicap races which were beaten in their latest handicap race at odds against and received the comment: *just failed, caught close home* or *caught post* would have resulted in 19 winners from 99 bets, a strike rate of 19% with a profit of 0.12.

The profit from both of these selection methods is on the low side which is to be expected given the difficulty associated with making any sort of profit at all from this race type and using a method based on conventional theory.

Effect of the Draw

The final, and most satisfying way to make the uniformity of the handicap work in our favour is through the draw.

The size and shape of Britain's racecourses varies enormously, from the small almost circular Chester to the figure of eight course at Windsor, unlike the *dirt tacks* of America which are all uniform in size and shape. One attribute the courses of both nations share though is the use of starting stalls. These were introduced in Great Britain in 1965 after continued pressure from the founder of the Timeform organisation, Phil Bull.

The aim of starting stalls is to produce an even break for all the animals, which is especially important over sprint distances. However, when horses are allocated a stall at the overnight declaration stage it also determines the part of the track over which they will run, near side, far side or centre, which can have a marked effect on the eventual race result. Obviously, the ultimate position of the horse relative to the other runners and the running rail is determined by the jockey, however the draw plays an important part in the positioning of the runners.

Water is not always retained uniformly across the width of the course and consequently has a detrimental effect to those animals running on the softer, or slower, side. Non-uniform water retention is especially apparent on cambered tracks with the lower part of the course retaining water for a longer period of time. Additionally, horses often run better, certainly straighter, when positioned close to the inside or outside rail, and furthermore, on round courses an inside draw will often mean the animal can take the shortest route from the starting stall to finishing line. All of the above factors can influence the outcome of the event with variable ground conditions becoming more significant in sprint races, since over longer distances the animals tend to bunch together thus minimising the effect of the softer ground.
Both the Sporting Life and Racing Post carry assessments of the draw although each paper only indicates whether high or low numbers have an advantage with the Racing Post illustrating the significance of the effect by including an additional factor on a scale of 1 to 10: ten implying a distinct advantage, one minimal advantage. *Raceform* also publish an analysis of the effect of the draw in the *official Formbook.*

So, assuming we know the advantage given by the draw and the strength of the bias (i.e. whether a specific draw has a pronounced or minimal effect) how can we make money from it? Firstly, we need to concentrate on non-juvenile handicaps. The reason for this is simple. The ability range of the animals in handicap races is normalised by the allocation of different weights by the BHB, therefore only a small external effect will make a noticeable change to the result of the race. In non-handicaps the ability range is likely to be much wider, and even with the best draw of the race and a ten lengths start a large proportion of the runners would still fail to win. In other words, the draw will not, in most cases, be a significant determining factor in non-handicaps, the crucial element being the ability of the horses. A similar argument can be applied to nurseries, although not to quite the same extent. Unexposed two-year-old horses are exceptionally difficult to handicap and therefore the differing abilities will not be accounted for as well as they are for older horses.

We now need to find the tracks with sufficient bias to ensure that we make a profit. This is not a straightforward task especially because the tracks with the most pronounced bias may not return a profit simply because the bookmakers are aware of this draw effect and will price the runners accordingly.

Since we are only betting in handicaps, we can make use of the race uniformity assumption previously discussed and used in the *Trainer Effect* section. Therefore, for each stall position over every race distance for every racecourse, we can calculate the expected number of winners and compare this with the actual number of winners and from this deduce the tracks with the necessary bias. Furthermore, by considering the average return per bet it is possible to determine which tracks will, in the long run, offer the best rate of return (i.e. those with a large bias which is not fully reflected in the prices on offer).

Based on an analysis of all courses in Great Britain, the following have been found to be sufficiently biased to make a selection process, based purely on this one factor, a profitable option:

Course	**Race Distance (f)**	**Draw**
Beverley	5	High
Catterick	7	High
Haydock	5	High
Kempton *(stalls stands' side)*	5	Low
Newbury *(round course)*	8	Low
Sandown *(stalls far side)*	5	High
Thirsk	5	High
York	10	Low

But how do we select, for example, the horse(s) to back in a 16 runner, 5 furlong sprint at Beverley?

The simplest approach is to back either the two horses drawn highest or lowest depending on the track bias regardless of other considerations. Over the period of analysis this would have resulted in 82 winners from 449 bets, a strike rate of just over 18% with a profit of 61p per £1 staked. A remarkable profit from such a simple betting approach. The strike rate, though, at a little over 18% is on the low side, this is because in each race we are backing two horses, and therefore the best achievable strike rate is only 50% (only one horse can win each race, dead-heats excluded).

Refining the Draw-Based Selections

In *Betting For A Living* Nick Mordin recommends backing the shortest priced of the three horses drawn highest or lowest according to the bias for specific tracks. But why back the shortest priced horse? All three benefit from the track bias, and given the uniformity of handicaps, one of the longer priced animals probably offers better value.

It is possible to improve on the strike rate and return given above, though, if we apply some of the principles we have already examined. Considering the starting price of the horse in its previous race, checking its most recent run was in a handicap and avoiding horses which start at 40/1 or more, all helps to improve the strike rate and average return. However, this has been covered in detail throughout this chapter so it is not necessary to reiterate it here.

The number of runners in the race, though, is worth discussing further. In very small fields, the effect of the bias will not be quite so crucial. For instance, in a four runner 5 furlong sprint at Haydock with the stalls on the stands' side, all the runners could be considered to be benefiting from the draw, with the *poorest* drawn horse (in stall 1) being only 2 or 3 yards from the favoured running rail. The larger the field the better, since an increasingly greater proportion of the runners will be suffering from a poor draw. However, from an analysis of the data, it has been found only races with seven or more runners should be considered for betting purposes.

One further consideration for betting on the draw is the style of running of the selection. It is important in sprints and races which are run on the turn in the first few furlongs to select horses with good early pace. A slow starting animal can lose a good position within a matter of strides and then have to round part or whole of the field to have any chance of winning, completely negating the positive effect of the draw. Naturally, it is difficult to tell whether the horse you are considering has *good early pace*, and this is just the type of woolly phrase I have tried to avoid throughout this text. In the absence of sectional timing, the next best guide is the comment-in-running for the animal's latest run, and I have found that it is good policy to avoid (or at least reduce the stake) for horses which were described as being *held up* or *starting slowly* in their last race.

Using the draw is a very powerful way of selecting horses, but with a strike rate of only 18% long losing runs are inevitable. There is also a tendency to ignore horses which were well beaten in recent races which can lead to missing good priced winners.

Summary

In this section we have applied different selection methods to races for non-juvenile horses. As with the juvenile runners, race times can provide an important guide to probable future success for older horses, especially those running in pattern races. Favourites are not normally considered to constitute a value bet, however, those racing against few opponents in non-handicaps at either end of the race distance scale seem to provide a good rate of return.

Non-juvenile handicap races have a unique status and possess qualities which enable the punter to get a good guide to the likely chance of success by simply considering the price the horse started for its most recent handicap race. In addition, it was found to be good policy to avoid handicappers which have recently been running in non-handicap races. Finally, the draw effect was analysed with the more profitable tracks highlighted.

PART II

BETTING ISSUES

BETTING ISSUES

If a man will begin with certainties, he shall end in doubts; but if he be content to begin with doubts, he shall end in certainties.

Francis Bacon (1605)

In this final section we examine several issues that are relevant to betting, most notably the concept of value. In addition, comparisons are made between Tote and starting price betting and between each way and win only bets. The section concludes with an analysis of forecast betting.

The Concept of Value in Betting

A great deal has been written about *value* in betting, with the arguments tending to fall into two classes. One argument states that value has no meaning in betting and the aim should be merely to back winners, regardless of price. The second view is slightly more scientific and states that value is determined from the relationship between price and probability of success. In other words, if you were offered 11/10 about the outcome of the toss of a fair coin, you should bet, if the price was less than evens you should keep your money safe and decline the offer.

The first argument is clearly absurd, and it is simple to demonstrate why. Take any period in your betting career when you made a profit, say a winning month or fortnight.

Now set the price of all the winners to 1/2 and recalculate your *profit*. I am confident that your former profit is now a loss. Do you still think that price is irrelevant?

The second argument is rather more difficult to illustrate. However, imagine you a walking along a street and a stranger offers you the chance to bet on the outcome of one toss of a coin he produces from his pocket. Furthermore, he offers you 3/1 about tails and 1/6 about heads. What do you do? In theory, you should take the 3/1 to all the money you have available and feel very satisfied. In practice, you would probably report this trickster to the authorities. Clearly, if someone if offering 3/1 about an even money chance they know more than we do.

This is the problem with horseracing. Unlike the toss of a fair coin, a horse race is a unique event never to be repeated, and we only know a small subset of the factors which have an influence on its result. With a fair coin we know everything relevant to the outcome, namely that the probability of it turning up heads is equal to the probability of it turning up tails. Therefore, a fair price about either outcome is evens. With a horse race it is not possible to be so accurate. Furthermore, we cannot repeat the same race time and time again in order to deduce the true probability of success for each horse from the results. This is, in fact, to our advantage. If it was possible to generate true probabilities of success about each horse, racing would simply turn into an equine version of roulette.

As an example of missing information, consider the case of Hopscotch. Hopscotch was a hurdler trained by Martin Pipe, and on 1 January 1991 was due to run in her eleventh race of the National Hunt season. Having already won nine of her previous ten races she started a short priced favourite (1/6, in fact) to beat three opponents. Peter Scudamore, Pipe's main jockey, was unable to ride that day, and instead commentated on the race for the BBC. Hopscotch looked unbeatable, as the price suggested. She had won over the course and distance, was suited by the going, had good (winning) recent form, was trained by a top trainer and ridden by one of the best National Hunt jockeys of all time, Richard Dunwoody. However, from the commentary box, Scudamore remarked that she had been fractious when loaded into the horsebox that morning, which was unusual and it could indicate that she was under par. This additional information only came to light minutes before the off, and bets had already been struck. Hopscotch finished third, beaten 6 lengths by 20/1 shot Master Dancer.

There are so many factors that effect horse races that it will always be impossible to evaluate the chances of each of the runners exactly. However, it is possible to calculate probabilities based on a known subset of factors. Conventionally, this has meant considering suitability of going, recent form etc., but is this the best subset of factors on which to base a profit making selection procedure? It certainly is the best information to use if you are trying to predict the most likely winner, but making a profit is a different matter.

Remember, that price is directly related to the perceived probability of success and within the price is embedded all these known factors as well as the bookmaker's margin. The reason the selection procedures throughout this book make good profits is simply because they were not constrained by preconceived ideas and were aimed at maximising the profit not the strike rate. If you want more winners and are not particularly worried about the profit level then use the conventional approach; if you want to make a real profit, change the emphasis of the way you assess races and make the objective profit, not winners.

So how does this help us with the value problem? Well, the concept of value is intrinsically tied to the selection process. Therefore, the value price for a horse selected using an appropriate selection method can only be deduced empirically. In other words, you have to consider whether backing similar horses with similar credentials at a similar price over several seasons would lead to a profit. This requires the gambler to keep detailed records of all his/her bets and if possible research similar races for several past seasons. These records should then be analysed and the profitable bets differentiated for the loss-making ones.

This analysis is crucial in determining whether your selection method has any merit to it. The selections should be broken down by price obtained and profit/loss totals calculated. You will probably find that, for a specific (profitable) selection method, when analysed by price the losses occur at the ends of the price scale i.e. for the very short priced horses and the long priced horses. The short priced animals are just under priced in relation to the selection method. A poor return from the long shots simply indicates that although you have found a good discriminating factor to highlight potential profit returning horses, it is not sufficient to overcome all the other factors which are working against your selection combined with the poorer price associated with these animals.

As an example, consider the selection method based on the draw effect. The average return is 61p per £1 staked. Given the simplicity of the method and the absence of other factors for consideration, it would seem logical that the longer the starting price the better the bet. However, after analysing the selections by starting price it was found that the horses starting at 40/1 or more only made a profit of 3p per £1 staked, which after taking tax into account is a loss. Therefore, we can conclude that horses optimally drawn and starting at 40/1 or more do **not** represent value.

The concept of value is very difficult to understand and even harder to explain. The important point, though, is to make the link with the selection method, and analyse previous races to isolate the value bets.

Each Way or Win Only Betting

Rather like the value problem, whether a punter should bet each way or straight win is dependent to a certain extent on the way the selection has been made. Therefore, to determine whether you should continue to place each way bets or not simply calculate your profit/loss from these bets from, say, the last twelve months. Then recalculate the bets as if they had been placed to win. From the two figures you can tell immediately if you would have been better betting to win.

From a more theoretical perspective, it is possible to calculate mathematically the return rates for win only and each way betting and thus determine the best betting strategy. As an example, let us consider a five horse race with no bookmaker overround (unrealistic but adequate for illustrative purposes). Therefore, we have five horses starting at 4/1, and putting £2 to win on each returns £10, the same as the total outlay. Now what of the each way bets? Staking £1 each way on the five runners incurs an outlay of £10, the return is given below:

From the winner: £1 at 4/1 and £1 at evens. **Return £7.**
From the second: £1 at evens. **Return £2.**

The total return from the each way bets is £9, which means that even in a fair book we have made a loss betting each way.

This loss is simply due to the each way fraction, which in the above example is ¼ of the odds. So, what fraction should be used in order to maintain the fairness of a zero overround book for each way betting?

At present the each way fraction varies according to the number of runners in the race and the race type and is given in Table 12:

Table 12: Each Way Fractions

Number of Runners	Race Type	Fraction	Places
2-4		*no place betting*	
5-7	Any	1/4	1,2
8+	Non-Handicap	1/5	1,2,3
8-11	Handicap	1/5	1,2,3
12-15	Handicap	1/4	1,2,3
16+	Handicap	1/4	1,2,3,4

Using the fair book example we can easily calculate the correct fractions for races with different numbers of runners. Listed in the tables below are the correct fractions for place betting:

Non-Handicap Races

Number of Runners	Current Fraction	Fair Fraction	Places
2-4	*no place betting*		
5	0.25	0.38	1,2
6	0.25	0.40	1,2
7	0.25	0.42	1,2
8	0.20	0.24	1,2,3
9	0.20	0.25	1,2,3
10	0.20	0.26	1,2,3
12	0.20	0.27	1,2,3
14	0.20	0.28	1,2,3
16	0.20	0.29	1,2,3
20	0.20	0.30	1,2,3
25	0.20	0.31	1,2,3

Handicap Races

Number of Runners	Current Fraction	Fair Fraction	Places
2-4	*no place betting*		
5	0.25	0.38	1,2
6	0.25	0.40	1,2
7	0.25	0.42	1,2
8	0.20	0.24	1,2,3
9	0.20	0.25	1,2,3
10	0.20	0.26	1,2,3
12	0.25	0.27	1,2,3
14	0.25	0.28	1,2,3
16	0.25	0.20	1,2,3,4
20	0.25	0.21	1,2,3,4
25	0.25	0.22	1,2,3,4

From the above tables we can see that for non-handicaps the current fraction of 1/5 for races of 8 or more runners represents very poor value, and as the number of runners increases the gap between the current and fair fraction widens meaning that the each way punter is receiving even poorer value.

For handicaps the picture is similar, although for races of 16 runners or more the current fraction is acceptable. Clearly, the worst case is a seven runner race when the fair fraction should be about 2/5, nearly double the current fraction of 1/4.

Therefore, each way betting seems to offer a poorer return than win only betting, except for handicaps of 16 to 20 runners where the fraction works in the punter's favour. But the best advice is to check your own bets and determine for yourself whether the each way bets you have placed previously have shown a better profit than if the bets had been struck win only, and then use this information to structure your future betting strategy.

Win Betting On The Tote

In the section covering Juveniles we briefly touched on the subject of Tote betting and decided that for the longer priced horses the Tote offered a better return on average. However, this is such an important area it is worth analysing the data a little more closely.

The Tote offers an alternative to the boards bookmakers with prices governed by a pool betting system. The dividend returned to the punter is therefore dependent on the number of winning bets and the total size of the pool. Consequently, anyone who bets on the Tote will not know what price their selection will be returned until after the race. With boards bookmakers a punter is able to take the price currently on offer. This is the reason that many punters shun the Tote in favour of bookmakers.

A comparison between Tote and starting price returns for over 2,000 races is given in the Table 13:

Table 13: Starting Price and Tote Return Comparison for Win Bets

	Average Difference Between Tote and SP†	
Starting Price	**Non-Handicaps**	**Handicaps**
Odds On	-0.03	-0.01
Evens-2/1	-0.09	-0.14
85/40-5/1	0.00	-0.08
11/2-10/1	0.41	0.69
11/1-16/1	4.00	4.76
18/1+	5.18	14.69
All	**0.51**	**1.51**

† the difference is calculated as Tote return minus starting price, therefore a positive figure indicates that the Tote return was higher.

Table 13 provides strong evidence for supporting the Tote. The average difference of 1.51 for handicap races is equivalent to receiving a free 6/4 winner with every winning bet placed. On closer inspection it can be seen that the Tote returns are generally higher for the longer priced horses i.e. 11/2 or greater. The longer priced horses tend to be under-bet by punters and consequently return a higher dividend on the Tote, however this lack of interest does not apparently result in inflated starting prices with the boards bookmakers (see Part I).

This is important information for punters who are unable to take an early price or early show about their selections. If you are betting at starting price, and your selection is likely to start longer than 11/2, it would seem sensible to bet on the Tote.

Dual Forecast or CSF

Forecast betting has become quite popular amongst betting shop punters. At present, punters can choose between the Computer Straight Forecast (CSF) and the Tote Dual forecast. The former bet requires the selected horses to finish first and second in the correct specified order before a payout is made, however, for the Tote Dual forecast bet the named selections need only fill the first two places, the order is irrelevant.

The return from the Tote Dual forecast is determined by a pool betting system and therefore the dividend is not known until after the race has been run. Whilst the CSF is not dependent on a pool system, the return will still be unknown until after the race due to the complex nature of its calculation which is based on, amongst other things, the overround of the race. However, it is possible to get a rough approximation of the likely return by performing the following calculation:

add one point to the starting price of the horse selected to finish second and multiply this by the starting price of the hoped for winner.

But how do the bets measure up in terms of value to the punter? Well, selecting horses at random and betting with the Tote Dual forecast would result in an average loss of 29p per £1 staked. The likely loss for the CSF is difficult to determine. However, in the book *How to Find Value When Betting*, Malcolm Howard estimates the loss per bet for the CSF to be in the region of 40p per £1 staked, before the tax component is added.

At 40p loss per £1 staked before tax, the CSF is on a par with the National Lottery with respect to return and, as such, should never be contemplated as a betting option. Therefore, when placing a forecast bet, I would always opt for the Tote Dual forecast.

Summary

This section has been devoted to general betting issues, the most important of which is the concept of value. Whilst this particular topic is extremely difficult to understand, it is crucial to betting. At the very least, punters should analyse their previous bets by price, in an attempt to discern which bets are profitable and which are losers in the long run. Each way betting is often thought of as a *safer* way to bet, however, we have seen that, for the majority of races, the expected return from each way bets is substantially lower than it is for win only bets. Again, punters should consult their previous each way bets and determine for themselves whether the selection methods employed are best suited by this form of betting. Tote win only betting was then suggested as a viable alternative to starting price betting when the likely price of the selection will be in excess of 11/2. Finally, avoid the Computer Straight Forecast, this bet should not be considered under any circumstances.